Literary Unlocking 2020
34 Short Steps Down the Staircase to Madness

Michael Gurner
The Sixty Second Scribe

First paperback edition November 2020

ISBN - 978-1-716-47243-5

Published by Sixty Second Publishing
www.sixtysecondscribe.com

Literary Unlocking 2020

Michael Gurner vividly remembers standing in John Menzies in Bletchley High Street at the age of 11 and reading the Author Blurb for The Restaurant at the End of the Universe by Douglas Adams. Michael remembers giggling both inwardly and outwardly at how funny it was and wondering why he'd never bothered to read any Author Blurbs before.

Michael made a personal commitment that from that day forward, he would read the Author Blurb of every book he read, to ensure that he missed out on no other such entertainment. It is sadly true that while he has kept to his pledge, he has yet to read a single Author Blurb that he would have regretted missing.

Anyway, Michael is descended from odd people and has always striven to ensure that he lives up to this ancestry - he is generally considered to have managed this well. He peaked early, with a poem about volcanoes entitled 'The Volcano' at the age of six that was met with significant maternal acclaim, and it's fair to say that he has been seeking similar recognition ever since. On rare occasions, he has managed to find people other than his mum who appreciate his work. He trusts that you may soon add yourself to this select list.

(He has also managed to avoid finding out what the proper name for Author Blurbs is for more than forty years now, and would appreciate it if people would stop emailing him about it. And Messaging, Whatsapping, Telegramming, Signalling and any other method you can currently think of or that has yet to be invented. Seriously. Stop it.)

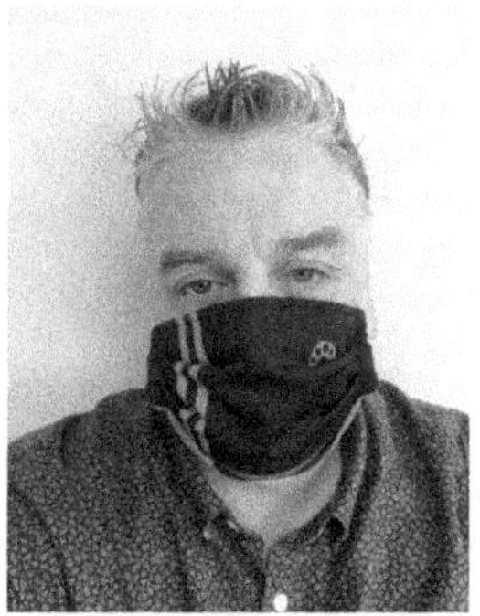

For anyone who's remotely controlled, as that might be interesting

Table of Contents

Literary Unlocking - 2020

Picture the scene – you're in the UK and you've seen the country ravaged by a pandemic that's affected the world, but that oddly seems to have affected the UK more than most. The country has been in some form of lockdown for five months or so and the talk in the media is turning to beginning the process of unlocking and returning to what may be left of 'normal'.

Running alongside that, we have, lucky as we are, the process of Brexit trundling along, deadlines coming and going and the few faint hopes of there being a sense of control somewhere, however minor, appear to be receding further and further from view.

Any sense of trust in those we have foolishly elected to lead us seems to have disappeared without a trace. They're just making this shit up as they go along, and lying without fear of repercussion on a daily basis. Which is nice.

So we're in the process of being told what is now safe to do, by people who we didn't trust in the first place, who are lying on a daily basis without an inkling of concern or shame, we have the highest death rates in the world and we're expecting that worse is still to come.

So what do you do? My answer is now familiar – I start writing - and this very tome is the latest output of that process. In a similar fashion to the Literary Lockdown poems that accompanied our descent into the madness of a national lockdown, this collection contains 34 individual poems, written, performed, recorded and published on 34 individual days in August and September 2020, spread across around 40 days in total.

I've given up pretending that I can always see the funny side in what's going on around me. I know it's there, and there are things that do make me laugh, but the anger that pours out of me at times is just overwhelming. That means that you might have to look pretty hard to find what I consider to be the funny side of some of the enclosed works, and you might have to be really prepared to work hard yourself at finding it funny too ☺. Alternatively, you can also go and watch the videos at www.sixtysecondscribe.com and watch the credits that accompany each recording – they're often a form of light relief from the frustrations of the day.

Having said that, there are light moments in here, some quite pretty moments, if I do say so myself, some cunning wordplay and some evocative imagery. At least that's what I think – you can let me know what you think when you've read it.

By definition, these works are of their time, and that time was very specific to the events in the news on the day that they were written. I think most/all of them stand up well without further context, but as these times are fast-changing, particularly as you may be reading this sometime after the events in question, should you need further context, then you'll find brief explanations of the drivers behind each work at the end of this collection.

Thank you for reading – stay safe.

Michael Gurner – The Sixty Second Scribe – November 2020

001 – Invading Hordes

Whatever your thoughts were on Brexit
And whether you're leave or remain
The one prize we know that we've won is
Control of our borders again.

So it's more than a little bizarre then to see
Our minister, uncomfortably smirking
While saying that without the help of the French
Our border controls just stop working.

It's ironic to see faces flushed and enraged
As the media stoke up the tension
Cos we've just turned our backs on existing accords
Including the Dublin convention

'We're standing alone – sovereign and proud
So fuck all your treaties and pacts!'
'But please will you help us and open your doors
So we can send 'unwanteds' back?'

Just one example of chaos to come
For our wilfully sleepwalking nation
As our media distract from the mess that we're in
By claiming the real threat's migration.

002 - Sack Race

MP in car that gets stopped by police
'Sack her' – soon trending on twitter
Stopped because her and the driver were black
Yet she's piled on by all the bullshitters

Ironic of course, is the following storm
It's explained at great length how she's wrong
That it wasn't their colour that prompted the stop
But that their car somehow didn't belong

'Our records show that your car's not from here'
Though that quickly was proved as untrue.
But would they have chosen, to look the plate up
Had the driver been Starmer, or you?

Lawrence, Macpherson and through to today
Institutional problems abound
The denial that such things could even exist
Means solutions are not being found

We should welcome the challenge from those with a voice
The baseline equation's at fault
Posh car plus black equals suspect
Can no longer remain the default.

Your grace under pressure's inspiring
So Dawn – solidarity sister
Keep using your platform for those with no voice
And together we'll fight the truth twisters

003 - Shameful Diversion

Have you ever seen anything worse?
Than the fucking BBC in a boat?
Watching a group of scared men and women
Bailing seawater to keep themselves afloat.

What do our proud broadcasters do? Do they help?
Do they lift them onto their own sturdy deck?
Or do they just point their cameras and hope for the worst
That those risking their necks will be wrecked.

So who here's the biggest threat to our lives?
The desperate souls afloat on the seas?
Or is it those with so little humanity
That they'll offer no help, with no hint of unease

Are these brave travellers the 'dangerous criminals'?
Described thus by our blustering PM
Or are they perhaps 'following the instincts of every parent'?
Which our cabinet deemed fine when it was one of them.

It's just a diversion. This isn't news.
Look away – ignore it – discount.
They want us discussing migration again
So we won't hold Johnson to account.

004 - That's the Role for Me!

Did you know that amongst all of the roles in our establishment
We now have a role called Clandestine Channel Threat Commander
Whose role appears to be to encourage people to drown
Instead of helping them. Like some twisted bystander

It made me think about the roles that we should have
What about a clandestine making people happy commodore
Or secretive chief in charge of keeping people safe and warm
Or undercover major in charge of general well-being and more

For some obscure reason, those would seem ridiculous
Some sort of distortion – a break from the norm
Yet let's be honest: they'd be far closer to what is needed
Than the ridiculous attempts to portray migrants as a swarm

So if we're going to create job roles to protect us in future
Let us create roles that offer some real support
Let us create roles that each of us would aspire to hold
Rather than one steeped in the worst kind of blood sport.

005 - From Refuge to Deluge

And so the heavens have opened
Thoughts turn from refuge to deluge today
And we're faced with some interesting questions
As today, it's my dear wife's birthday

Do we tell people 'stay away from our garden!'?
That rain has indeed now stopped play?
I'm English, so I worry that's presumptuous
They might not have planned to anyway.

Cross our fingers and hope for the best
That people will know not to descend?
If they do, we'll just talk on the doorstep?
And hope that we'll still remain friends.

Do we put the gazebo up
In the garden, in the rain?
So we can sit under a gazebo
In the garden, in the rain?

Or do we just shrug our shoulders
And say 'well if we were working together'
Or if it was a pub, this'd all be ok
So come in – get out of the weather.

006 - Eh? Levels

Work hard.
Work yourself into self-harm.
No apologies for raising the alarm.
Put simply, you're betting the farm.

You work hard.
And then. You get a U. A U.
And the craziest thing that you're left to chew?
That U is nothing to do with you.

You got a U
Cause four years ago someone else got a U
Not you. A different child at your school. Got a U.
And therefore – so do you.

This system.
That favours those from private school
Is fair and robust. Says our blustering fool
The 20th Eton prime minister. How cruel.

So let us.
Let us sack Gavin Williamson – it's his responsibility
Let us fight for a system not serving nobility
Let us apologise to our kids with appropriate humility.

They deserve better than this.

007 – Jail Them Today

The misplaced belief 'mongst our leaders
That staff safety's best left to bosses
Puts decisions right in the hands of
Those who'll earn more if they avoid losses

Making business responsible for safety
Is like putting the Tories in charge of protecting the NHS
Oh.
Anyway…

300 staff at a Northampton firm
Tested positive for the virus this week
Yet we meekly accept it as 'one of those things'
No challenge or legal critique

How can that happen? Please – tell me do?
'Less the guidelines we're given are wrong
That business cannot have adhered to them
And the consequences have to be strong.

Drag leaders of that firm in front of a judge
And make them explain it today
And if they have failed in their duty of care
Then jail them until they obey.

The reason that we have employment laws?
Business works on dollars and cents
The conflict 'tween profit and safety of staff
Means failure must have consequence.

008 – Well That's All Sorted Then

Sometimes it's hard to know just where to start
It's hard to pry all of this chaos apart
But pry it we must, with all of our hearts
The stakes are now simply too high

A major change published on Twitter at night
Through a courtesan press with no backbone in sight
While the A level scandal continues to bite
Distraction or something more sly?

So Hancock is blaming the PHE team
For following his orders, least that's how it seems
So now he engenders a brand new regime
In the hope that this one will comply

So who will be holding the reins in its place?
The woman who failed running our track and trace
They must find it hard to maintain a straight face
In the face of the public outcry

That Harding, Gardiner, Doyle and Hancock
Should blame PHE shouldn't come as a shock
If it wasn't so serious, t'would be easy to mock
But for now, I'll just keep asking why.

009 – That's Not A Virtue

You hold the reins of power
There are experts all around
But you ignore them all and
When it fails, you double down

In case you need some clarity
To help you think this through
Ignoring those with expertise
Is neither strength nor virtue

The u turn that this ends in
Won't address all the effects
The world you're playing games in
Is too intricate and complex

Your experiment has failed.
You're hurting people.
Step down
Now

010 – Fed Up with Being Fed Up

It's too easy.
And at the same time
It's too hard.

I sit and think
What shall I write now
Too much choice

I want to write
Something uplifting
But I'm cross.

Cross all the time
And I think I need
To stop that

So here's a joke:

How many Tories
Does it take
To change a lightbulb?

A spad or two to decide to remove the existing lightbulb
A courtesan journalist to break the news on twitter at 10pm
A handful to invent something that doesn't give off any light, but
that matches some weird ideological position that they have.
A civil service who are asked to force this thing that isn't a lightbulb
into the socket
A minister to categorically state that the new approach is exactly
what is needed
A prime minister to shout about the benefits of darkness
A minister to categorically state that darkness is the future and
won't be changing

A minister to announce that the policy has been dropped
A civil service to mop up the problems caused by all of the above.

I'll have them rolling in the aisles.

011 – Viva La Revolución

Are the youth as angry as I am?
The over 50s can't lead the revolt
Much as I'd love to be leading the way
We'd end up wheezing and calling a halt

You don't want to storm the winter palace
And find you need to pause
To get help for those left behind
Not fit enough to fight for the cause

We're relying on you.
The young will have to lead.
But lead and we will follow
Just perhaps not at top speed

012 – Where's Johnson?

Trump is unravelling before us
There's no speeches weirder than his
But the American's have an advantage
They know where their lunatic is.

So please fellow citizens assist us
Please help find our blustering Caesar
Check out your kitchens and garages
Case he's trapped in your fridge or your freezer.

013 – Stable Situation

300 cases – single workplace
Yet it took a week
Before the business closed its doors
Which seems a little weak

Credit where it should be due
I guess I must endorse
They've finally shut the stable door
Now where the hell's that horse.

014 – Cabinet Search Party

I have a plan.
We've been looking at this all wrong.
Don't look to end the hide and seek
Instead, seek to prolong

Send the cabinet searching
Do you see what that could mean?
Get the full advantage
By switching to sardines!

As each one uncovers him
They hide with him and hence
We rid ourselves of all of them
Now THAT is common sense.

015 – Shakespearean Summer

Perturbed at how hard it has been to adjust
To the absence of trust in the man we entrust
As he lies without thought of the growing disgust
As the mistruths and spin speed along.

Everything's framed as a media event
Fed propaganda, we're left to lament,
As we crawl through the summer of this con's tent,
That the winter ahead 'twill be long.

016 – Capitalist Death Throes

Economically speaking, there are greater concerns
Than the pandemic's impact on corporate returns
Automation and AI will top all of our concerns
As capitalism struggles with its plunder

The killer question isn't 'how will robots pay their dues?'
Instead it's 'how will robots buy the products you produce?'
And if you don't 'produce', then I've got some sadder news
You won't be safe as all is torn asunder

The thing to watch for now is the pandemic situation
Used to justify increased employment terminations
But they won't rehire instead they'll seek to widen automation
The lightning strikes while we await the thunder.

017 – God Save Our History

First of all, communal singing's something 'off the list'
If you're irate 'bout land of hope and glory, please desist
In the wider scheme of things, I couldn't give a toss
There's far more pressing things bout which you should be getting
cross

But if you want to prod at it, then here's the thing to muse on
The excesses of our past are things we all should have a view on
Historical abuses have an impact on today
And without the proper education, that won't go away

Should we be singing songs that blindly glorify our past?
Not until we've dealt with all the questions left unasked.
It's not distorting history to share the truths of old
Or politicising, as the National Trust's been told

It's being honest 'bout the things that got us where we are
That allows adult debate 'bout all we find in our memoirs
As an atheist republican who's prone to vent his spleen,
If I was going to ban a song, I'd start with God Save The Queen.

018 – Who Do You Think You Are Kidding?

You've got to hand it to them – they know just who their base is
They point dad's army graphics at their angry reddened faces
They tell them that their problems are all caused by other races
And say the EU stops us from deporting all these cases.

The pesky lawyers share their ire – their 'activist' endeavours
Have angered those who don't respect the rule of law whenever
It stops them doing what they want, and so they seek to sever
The rights afforded all of us that should be ours forever.

And so we have a government disrespecting rule of law
Alluding to invasion, hinting back to bloody wars
Suggesting all will be ok, once laws they can ignore
So please consider when it will be you they're coming for.

019 – Home Office Corridors

There are direct links to be made that's for sure
Tween the home office shouting 'bout asylum wars
And Britain First thugs out to settle their scores
Harassing away in hotel corridors

We're creating conditions where goons of this sort
See government policies offering support
To the ideological fictions they're taught
As they draw up their lists of who's next to deport

Encourage the right and there'll be consequences
It emboldens their type towards greater offences
So let's move our arses from atop of these fences
And recall what the most useful form of defence is.

020 – A Nightingale Sang in Trafalgar Square

I've seen some unexpected sights
But none more odd this year
Than anti-mask protestors shouting
'Freedom' with a cheer.

No to masks, vaccines and second wave
Seemingly oblivious at
The contradictions between those three
And how together they might influence that

In the cold light of the day
They may rue that they were there
If they booked their place in The Nightingale
As they sang in Trafalgar Square.

021 – Socialist Irker

You're quite the little warrior
You'll hunt through ancient tweets
To find a hint of anything
To throw at Corbyn's feet

And yet you're somehow muted
No need felt to chastise
When thugs unfurl a fascist flag
Right before your eyes

Your silence echoes loudly
And a nagging doubt persists
It's not fascists that irk you
Sounds more like socialists.

022 – Slow News Day

With everything that's going on
At home and overseas
Covid and disturbances
Protestors on the streets

Our media must prioritise
'Tween all the sorry tales
How they will inform us and
Remove ophthalmic scales

Today they have excelled themselves
In choices that they've made
Everywhere I look it's there
Garishly displayed

In print, tv and internet
Not civil war or crime
But the cost of plastic bags in shops
Will increase in eight months' time.

023 – Halley's Ice Cream Van

Just as you've finally cracked it
You've mastered the script – every word
Every syllable read with distinction
The appropriate intention inferred

The pace and the energy's gorgeous
Articulate, clear, ah but then
That freakishly noisy ice cream van
Means you have to record it again.

024 – A Little Rashford

I was chatting to my mum last night
As I do pretty much every night. Right?
She asked me why I wasn't giving attention
To Marcus Rashford who surely deserve a mention

And my immediate response was that I'd prefer
To use my platform instead to transfer
The opprobrium to those who've actually felicitated
And thereby whose actions have surely necessitated. it.

But she's right. I should celebrate those who choose.
To use their platform to deal with issues
That the rest of us just choose to embrace
As part of how we do things in this place.

So Marcus, I celebrate you. I do.
You're everything that we should be aspiring to.
And I'm happy to cheer you and hope you overcome.
Especially as it will help to placate my mum.

025 – Rogue Trader

He's anti-same sex marriage
But I don't want you to be alarmed
He's actually fond of climate change
Thinks it's doing us more good than harm

So ignore that he's inappropriate
His misogyny clearly displayed
Forget he's a raving homophobe
Cos he's also an expert in trade.

026 – Unplanned Complexity

We've all met their type, although usually at work
They make huge decisions that drive you berserk
And their lack of respect for your expertise pains
As you know that they'll do it again and again.

But now we can see deadlines not being met
Our entire economic success under threat
The labelling debacle looks like just one instance
As their arrogance tears up the rules in an instant

We seem to have lost the most basic foundations
We've handed the reins of our struggling nation
To people who honestly don't understand
That some stuff's too complex to be left unplanned

027 - Sunblocked

Extinction rebellion are back in the news
And today more than ever, they've got me amused
They're forcing the climate debate to the fore
And they're right in your face, where they can't be ignored

They're quite unconventional, hence they have haters
Yet the numbers supporting them grow ever greater
But perhaps the most beautiful thing that they've done
Is to fight climate change by blocking The Sun

028 – Ermine or Vermin

I saw a dying rat this week.
I first presumed it dead.
I poked it gently with a broom
It squealed, then slowly fled.

I felt a wave of pity
As this rodent met its mort
How could loathsome vermin
Make me want to give support

And that seemed so analogous
It's the moral of this story
As it might provide a reason why
Some people still vote Tory .

029 – Waiving Britannia

Massive increase in Covid infections
So starts the familiar loop
Later that evening, a Sunday again,
A newspaper picks up a scoop

We're ripping up Brexit agreements we've made
I've no clue if that's at all true
But the one thing I do know that's not a surprise
The infections are knocked down the news

If it's true, then it's reckless and shows that once more
We're treating the EU as fools
And I'm kind of ashamed to see once again
Britannia is waiving the rules.

030 – Specifically Limited

At least it's becoming more open
They no longer feel they should hide
They're planning unlawful decisions
By which we will have to abide

But maybe it has some advantage
This lack of respect for the law
Let's make this the back of the camel
And this woeful approach, the last straw

I'll do some shoplifting this weekend
And decide just what taxes I'll pay
As breaking the law's ok if it's in
A specific and limited way.

031 – Six Appeal

Six people. That sounds nice and easy.
The rules are now clear once again!
That doesn't apply when at work though
Or at school, in a church, or a plane.

I don't understand why family and friends
Are the clear and predominant dangers
And are apparently more of a threat to me
Than my colleagues and massed unknown strangers.

If a choice must be made between family and work
Then I've got the answer – a winner
I'll just work from home, say bollocks to Pret
And have a big family Christmas dinner.

032 – Parliamentary Palaver

All this palaver would make much more sense
For a new government, there'd be some defence
But this isn't that.

This is a government who promoted this bill
Who broke UK law to avoid scrutiny of this bill
This is the outcome of that.

They won an election championing legislation
That now they pretend was not of their creation
There's no excusing that.

This is an idiot. Arguing against himself.
That's it. No rhymes, no jokes, no punchlines.
Stop him. He's a twat.

033 – It's All About Prioritisation

At number one in the Beeb's
6 o clock news headlines
Difficulty getting tests
For those with worrying signs

At two, it's that mingling
With friends could break the law
At three the unemployment rise
A real concern for sure

At four the shocking news that
Zoe Ball is earning more
While Lineker is earning less
That cannot be ignored

That's all pretty serious stuff
It's obvious why they'd choose
To prioritise those crucial things
Above less important news

Humanity at a crossroads
Our species might not survive
Says major report on biodiversity
Which scrapes in at number five

034 – Not Moving On

Peeking out the window
Counting those attending
Phone clutched tightly in your hand
'Case behaviour needs amending

It's for the public good you see
The interests of the nation
We're all in this together
Whatever the duration

But when our dear old government
Had the chance to show they meant it
They changed the rules so Cummings
Got let off, and I resent it

Much as you would like us all
To move on and let that go
I can't. I won't.
And I'm not alone.

Notes

001 – Invading Hordes

I'm chuckling slightly at this, mainly because just a few months later, it already seems so very mild and light-hearted. This was the start of what has become a concerted campaign by our government to demonise anyone seeking a better life here, while doing everything possible to distract from the fact that the treaties they've ripped up as part of the Brexit process played a significant part in helping us to exercise control over it. I might be wrong, but my guess is that this is one of the very few poems that reference the Dublin Convention ;). Underneath all of this of course, is a compliant media allowing themselves to be manipulated and enabling attention to be directed away from government failings.

002 - Sack Race

A pleasant break from the rigours of the pandemic and Brexit, as MP Dawn Butler was a passenger in a car that was pulled over by police. The police then chose to twist themselves into a whole mess of explanations as they tried to come up with an explanation that didn't read 'we're suspicious of black people in decent cars'. They failed.

003 - Shameful Diversion

Not sure I've been as appalled as I was at this, even with everything that's going on at the moment. I watched a BBC news crew that took itself into the middle of the channel and filmed migrants, bailing water out of the flimsiest of dinghies. Our beloved state broadcaster chose to offer no help or support, but just to point their cameras at these terrified people. Sensationalist tabloid 'reporting' of the worst possible variety and I felt ashamed. Why they didn't help them, or at least just stay on the beach and wait for them if they realised that they wouldn't be able to help them, I will never understand.

004 - That's the Role for Me!

This is pretty much what it says on the tin – we've decided that what's missing in these troubled times is a ridiculously-named role whose function appears to be to find ways to make brown people drown, in the hope that that will discourage others from following them. We should be better than this.

005 - From Refuge to Deluge

This was an interesting moment, in that for the first time since the lockdown started, as a family, we found ourselves in a situation where we wanted to see relatives, but the weather was unlikely to make that sensible outside. I don't mean it was the first time we'd wanted to see relatives, but it was the first specific event where it had been a thing. It was an interesting situation where following recently relaxed lockdown regulations, it would have been fine for us to meet with friends or family in a pub, but it wouldn't have been ok for us to meet them in our house, whatever distancing approach we chose to take, or however careful we were. It was a perfect example of how the rules that are in place at any point in time, have to stand up to some level of scrutiny, as if they don't, people will do their own thing. We sat in our garden, under a gazebo, in the pouring rain.

006 - Eh? Levels

If there was an example of a government that were just blundering along, making things up as they went along, then this was it. I'd like to think it was perhaps the first point where those leading us may have started to question their 'there's nothing we can't explain away afterwards' approach, and had begun to consider that some things might actually benefit from planning and expertise. The A Level fiasco was unfair on our kids, was completely predictable and could be seen coming a mile off. Not our finest hour.

007 – Jail Them Today

There's an underlying theme in a lot of the Tory approaches to dealing with the pandemic, with Brexit or just about anything else, which I'd summarise as being 'everyone can rely on businesses to do the right thing by their staff'. I don't mean to knock any individual businessperson, but that has rarely been my experience in my dealings with businesses. The public had been told to return to work and that their businesses would look after them, which asked for a lot of trust that had not necessarily been earned up to that point. And then one business had 300 staff test positive for the virus in a single week. That can only have been because either the guidelines themselves were wrong, or in this case that business had not been following them, yet no action was taken. I still don't understand why.

008 – Well That's All Sorted Then

As the nation slowly unlocked itself, and we began to look back a little on what had happened during the previous few months, our dear Health Secretary decided that, despite all evidence to the contrary, it was Public Health England as a body, that was responsible for us having the worst death rates in the world. That's Public Health England that reports into the Health Secretary. Of course the private sector was then asked in to manage its replacement, and the reins were handed to the woman who had overseen repeated failures in our track and trace approach. Lovely.

009 – That's Not A Virtue

It is widely accepted that there is a principle being followed by our government ministers that says simply 'admit no failings'. Whatever happens, however wrong things go, they are met with public denials of both responsibility for an issue, and even that the issue exists at all, however much reality may contradict that. The justification seems to be, that this is actually some sort of strength that will see us all through difficult times, however all it really does is further undermine trust in the government/scientists/everything at a time when it is so crucial that we can trust those in power.

010 – Fed Up with Being Fed Up

I'm chuckling at this one all over again – I was fed up with being so cross all the time, so decided to tell a joke instead. Twitter really loved this one, which I'm naïve enough to take as a positive.

011 – Viva La Revolución

There are lots of people wondering if there's anything that would be enough to make the Great British public rise up and revolt. You might consider it rather odd, but I was surprised at just how late the self-realisation has come that I might not be young enough to lead it myself.

012 – Where's Johnson?

Johnson had pretty much disappeared at this point, so this was a simple call back to one of the Literary Lockdown poems. I liked this because it allowed me to reference Johnson's supposed classical background and rhyme it with his favourite hiding place.

013 – Stable Situation

A second factory with 300 cases in a single week, yet it took a week to close the factory. Seemed crazy to me then. Still does now.

014 – Cabinet Search Party

Johnson was still missing, so I proposed a way to use this to our advantage. If you're not familiar with Sardines, it's a variation on hide and seek where when you find someone, you climb in with them, which continues until all but one person is hiding together.

015 – Shakespearean Summer

Johnson had finally been tracked down to a tent in a remote part of Scotland, although most of the evidence suggested that this was probably fabricated, and that he'd been on a Russian oligarch's yacht that was moored nearby. Anyway, this was really just an excuse to make a very poor pun.

016 – Capitalist Death Throes

I'd been reading Aaron Bastani's Fully Automated Luxury Communism and was dwelling on just what that could mean for our futures, irrespective of the pandemic that continued around us. There was an exchange referenced in the book between a union leader and Henry Ford junior (I think it was them anyway – forgive me if I'm remembering incorrectly) about the impact of automation on the workforce, and the relevance of it to our current situation really grabbed me. My guess is that businesses will never re-recruit to the level they were at prior to the pandemic, and that the pandemic will in effect be used as cover for restructuring that they would never have had the public support to do without it.

017 – God Save Our History

The press was full of 'Rule Britannia Banned – it's Political Correctness Gone Mad' type headlines, as it had been announced that Rule Britannia would not get its traditional annual singalong at the end of Last Night of the Proms. The fact that there was unlikely to be an audience to sing, and that if there was, then singing had been identified as a major spreader of the virus, seemed to have been forgotten amongst the hysteria. A perfect example of a non-story managing to keep real news out of the headlines.

018 – Who Do You Think You Are Kidding?

Our beloved Home Office, under the command of our smirking Home Secretary, released a video attacking refugees that was wrong on so many levels. It used graphics reminiscent of Dad's Army (no way was that an accident) to engender some sort of wartime invasion fear. It attacked lawyers upholding the law as activists and it wrongly blamed the EU for us not being able to just 'send them back', announcing proudly their intentions to restrict human rights as soon as we'd fully left the EU. Had someone like Farage done this a few years ago there would have been outrage – that it's now just business and usual for our Home Office speaks volumes about how far and how quickly we've sunk.

019 – Home Office Corridors

As if by magic, as the government ramps up their anti-immigration rhetoric, so the extreme right wing in the UK take their cue and see it as a green light. In this case, Britain First thugs were roaming the corridors of a hotel where refugees were being housed, knocking on doors and filming the confused and scared individuals who answered.

020 – A Nightingale Sang in Trafalgar Square

One of the stranger things over the course of the summer has been the rise of 'anti-maskers' as a thing. They've had a number of demonstrations where they've been parading around, unmasked, and failing to observe any social distancing. This was a pun on the wartime song by Maschwitz and Sherwin, although I have no idea whether it was too obscure for most people to get.

021 – Socialist Irker

At the anti-mask demonstration in Trafalgar square, we saw, for the first time that I can remember, the British Union of Fascists publicly unveiling their flag. That they feel emboldened enough to do this is concerning, but what I found most telling was that those who had spent the last five years or so trawling through every previous utterance of anyone to do with the left of the labour party, seeking anything that if you looked at it in a certain light, and from the right angle, could possibly be construed as anti-Semitic, those people were totally silent and presumably unbothered by the unveiling of a fascist flag in the middle of our capital. Intriguing.

022 – Slow News Day

This was rather surreal – with everything that's going on in the world - on this day, the lead item pretty much everywhere I looked, was that the price of plastic bags in shops was going to rise in eight months. I could find no logical reason why this was considered news, and why it was so prominent on that date. But it was bloody weird.

023 – Halley's Ice Cream Van

I can't actually remember what I had originally written for this day. I know I'd come up with something that I was relatively pleased with and had sat down to record it, only to find that every time I pressed record, an ice cream van in the streets around my house would merrily chime away and destroy my recording. So in the end it seemed more sensible to write about that instead – I don't think the Comet analogy stood up to too much scrutiny, but I liked the idea of the world dreading the arrival of an ice cream van, just as I was dreading it destroying my recordings.

024 – A Little Rashford

Marcus Rashford – top bloke. My Mum – eternally positive. She bullied me into it basically. It did make me ponder on how to be more positive in what I publish. At least for a day or two.

025 – Rogue Trader

I've lost the ability to see past my own cynicism a lot of the time, but I had this down as a 'distraction story that will never come to pass' moment. Former Australian PM Tony Abbott had been mooted as a UK trade envoy who would be helping us to secure all these marvellous trade deals that were just waiting to be signed in our exciting post-Brexit world. I'll be honest, I knew very little about him, but a brief google around and you find out that he's got some really questionable views on women, sexuality and the environment, which just reinforced my view that they were putting him up there as a decoy, so they could announce Rolf Harris or someone similar. Of course, it turned out that we appointed Tony Abbott.

026 – Unplanned Complexity

This was about yet another example of the lack of attention to detail that bedecks the Brexit process – it had suddenly come to public attention that the deadline for us to agree just how we would need to label food exports to the EU from January 1st 2021 had passed, leaving yet more uncertainty in our very near futures.

027 – Sunblocked

I did enjoy this, and it was one where I stole the punchline from someone on twitter (I can't remember who it was, but I did credit them in the video credits – I'm nice like that). Extinction Rebellion had blockaded three major printworks where the majority of UK newspapers were printed, leading to a lack of newspapers, a lot of whining and a whole lot of publicity.

028 – Ermine or Vermin

This was very literal – I had seen a dying rat in my garden, and I was genuinely surprised at the level of sympathy I felt for it. I was also genuinely impressed that I managed to use it to have a go at the Tories ☺.

029 – Waiving Britannia

In one of a long, long series of government policy announcements made, not in a public briefing, or to the House of Commons, but instead made on Twitter at 10pm on a Sunday night, the government let it be known that they would not be honouring the withdrawal agreement or political declaration that they had forced through the commons less than 12 months before.

030 – Specifically Limited

As the world looked on with a mix of amusement and concern, we had a minister stand up in parliament and explain that we were indeed going to break international law, implying that it was acceptable because we would be breaking it in a specific and limited way. This is truly through the looking glass stuff isn't it?

031 – Six Appeal

Johnson decided that all of the rules that he'd put in place so far were too complex, and he announced with some fanfare that they would all be replaced by a 'rule of six'. The rule of six said that you could meet with a maximum of six people, pretty much anywhere you liked, which was indeed more straightforward. Except that it didn't apply to workplaces, schools, churches, planes or a whole host of other places. What wasn't provided was any evidence or explanation as to why our family and friends were now more dangerous than colleagues or strangers, which made the whole thing a little weird.

032 – Parliamentary Palaver

This was the point at which it became (almost) impossible to lampoon Johnson and his crew. They were standing up and berating a bill that they wrote, that they promoted, that they broke UK Law to avoid parliament being able to apply proper scrutiny of, that they had won an election with this bill as the focus of their policy platform and they were somehow now pretending it was nothing to do with them, and that the detail of the bill wasn't strong enough.

033 – It's All About Prioritisation

I sat open-mouthed as the headlines came up on the telly for the evening news. The threat to the survival of our species just scraped in at number five.

034 – Not Moving On

The government were asking people to phone the police if they saw their neighbours breaking the new lockdown rules, suggesting again that we're all in this together. Yet Cummings, and those who supported him when he broke the rules, still stand. I'm not moving on. I can't.